# Top 10 Passive Income Ideas In 2020

**MOHAMMED KASMI**

# Contents

1. INTRODUCTION
2. YouTube
3. Digital Products
4. Print On Demand
5. Affiliate Marketing
6. Online Courses
7. Merchandise
8. Royalties
9. Stock Media
10. E-books / Audiobooks
11. CONCLUSION

# INTRODUCTION

Hello everyone in this book you will learn about passive income streams and how you can apply some of them yourself to earn money while you sleep.

It's worth noting that this book is not for people who are lazy or into get rich quick schemes because this is going to require actual work. But I'm gonna tell you exactly how to do it.

So without further ado let's dive deep into the subject at hand and discover 10 Ways to Make Passive Income Online.

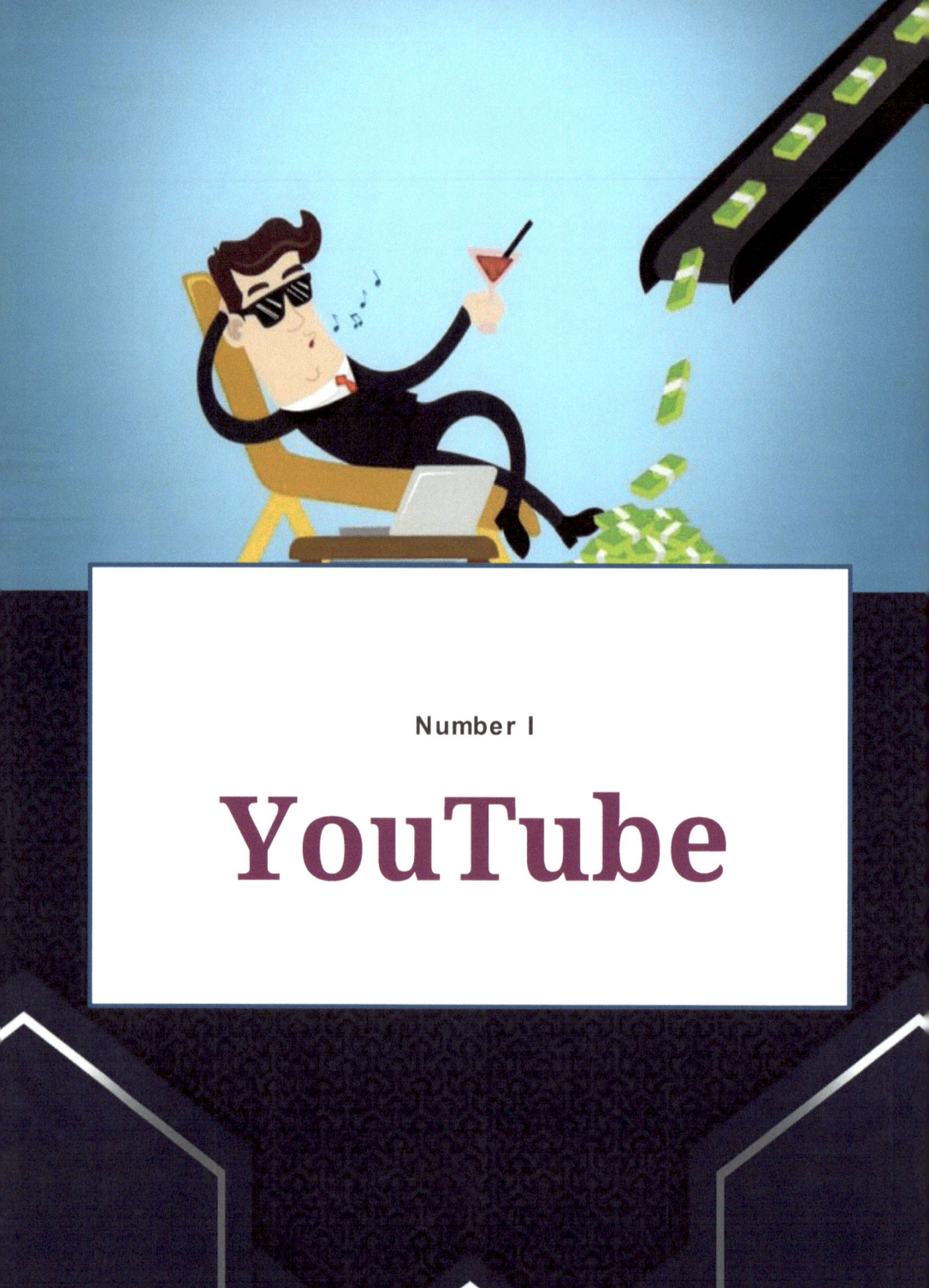

**Number I**

# YouTube

# YouTube

Obviously, you probably realize the importance of YouTube when it comes to building a passive income stream.

You can literally make a video today that will make you hundreds of dollars in passive income for the next few years,

So by putting the effort upfront and creating quality content you can be earning 100$ per day for the lifetime of your channel

Isn't that nice?

Also, the good thing about YouTube is that you don't have to rely on AdSense to generate this income.

You can add affiliate links to your videos and earn money that way, or sell your own merch…etc.

There are a lot of ways to earn money from YouTube and because videos are there forever you can leverage this and create an income stream that gets you passive money each single day.

Number II

# Digital Products

# Digital Products

One of the best ways you can make passive income online is your own direct product sales and when I talk about this, in this case, I'm talking about digital products.

Do you know why digital products are amazing?

Well one, you can make a lot of money every month with all the digital products that you make. It also keeps you independent.

By making a digital product, you have very little overhead.

There are so many different places where you can make digital products.

Websites like gumroad / sellfy / kajabi...etc. all allow you to make digital products and sell them.

It's just a matter of what platform you like and your budget
(some are a bit expensive).

Now, as for the kind of products you can sell :

You can sell graphics packs / a digital course / a video template...etc.

Whatever you are passionate about, the sky is the limit.

If you wanted to go and do something just a little bit more tangible, then I would say you could do print on demand products.

Number III

# Print On Demand

# Print On Demand

With print on demand you create a design and print in on physical products whenever you sell one.

The advantage of print on demand is that there are a lot of websites where you don't need to have an inventory or anything, all you need is to upload a design to those website and they will print the design on the product and ship it whenever a customer orders one
Hence the name "Print on Demand".

There a lot of websites where you can sell print on demand products :
There's : Zazzle / Teespring / Redbubble / Threadless / Merch By Amazon / Teepublic...Etc.

You can make some decent passive income with print on demand, but I personally like digital download products a little bit more because the margins are better.

When I make a digital download product, I keep more than 95% of all of the money on that product because of how cheap it is to host it on that other platform, okay?

But if you want to do something else and you want to do like posters and other print on demand products then you should look into that.

The margins will not be as good on that but it is something that you can do.

And a lot of you will think I need to build an audience to accomplish that but you should be doing that no matter what anyway.

In the age of social media, building an audience is free and that's free website traffic.

Now, if you don't feel you have the skills to do print on demand products because maybe you don't have a background in design or illustration, you have another option.

You can actually do what's called Affiliate Marketing,

Number IV

# Affiliate Marketing

# Affiliate Marketing

So, with affiliate marketing, you can sell someone else's product and you can get a commission.

So, you can get the sales and it's really convenient because you can use a website like Amazon and you can get affiliate revenue commissions there.

Problem with something like Amazon, though, is you're gonna only get like two to 4% usually on average on that affiliate program. But there are better programs out there that pay higher commissions.

Amazon just has the most robust offering of diverse products for whatever genre, niche, or hobby or expertise that you're dealing with or whatever audience you're dealing with. That's why so many people go to it.

But if you go into very specific categories, for example, if you're somebody that's either in websites, web hosting, web design, or online business or ecommerce, you can do stuff with web hosting companies.

There are people who do affiliate marketing with Wix and Bluehost that can make anywhere from $85 to $100 dollar plus commissions on every one of those sales, so, in terms of making $100 dollars a day, that's really straightforward because it translates to a single transaction or at least two transactions to accomplish that.

But also, for people that are into other niches like for example the YouTube niche, there's another affiliate program that some use called Epidemic Sound.

It's a service that provides background music to content creators.

It's for the royalty stock music that people are able to use as online content creators and that's $30 dollars per sale for a 30 day free trial.

So, if people sign up for a 30 day free trial, you'd get a commission on that and it's a pretty nice commission for what it is.

So, if three people use any of the links in the videos that you've made, you'd have the opportunity to make a $30 dollar sale there.

So, again, if you find the right affiliate program for your niche, it can be a lucrative opportunity and it may not be that challenging. Even with a small audience, if it is the right audience, to do $100 dollars a day.

Now, here's where that gets into an interesting way to make passive income.

So far we talked about affiliate sales, but let's now talk about referral sales.

You might be thinking, aren't those the same thing? No, they're not!

Because you see, what I mean with this is if you have your own digital download product, you can have your own affiliates and so you're making referral sales.

So the way that that would look is : let us assume that somebody was an affiliate for you and you gave him a 30% commission on a $100 dollar product.

If that product is sold at full price with no coupons for $100 dollars and somebody is getting a 30% referral commission on that, then guess what happens?

Without you doing the work of making the sale, you still get $70 dollars and they get 30.

So, if you build a digital product and you do referral commissions with your own affiliates, you're making the majority of the money on their sales, you own the product, you own the brand, they're just operating as a sales force for you and it's not like you're paying them hourly for that, you're paying them only on the sales they make.

So, again, referral sales are very lucrative to you as someone who owns a product and so, this kind of leads into another way of making passive income.

**Number V**

# Online Courses

# Online Courses

In addition to having your own digital download products, if you are skilled at something, you can make a course for it and that's another passive income stream that you could make.

This tie directly to digital products because the more products you have between, making a digital product, and making an online course.

That's a product that you own and having those referral sales puts money back in your pocket for somebody else making the sale for you and reaching an audience that you may not have.

So, again, if you are struggling to build an audience or you would like to access someone else's audience, those referral sales are a good way for you to make more money.

That's how you can scale your business.

Speaking of building an audience, building an audience on YouTube gives you access to the YouTube partner program where you can make passive income through advertising.

So, usually I say that passive income means building a product-based business but it could also be building a content-based business if you're gonna leverage advertising placements and spots.

Now, there are a couple of ways to think about this:

You can also do this with a podcast,

By the way, it's just easier in general to do it with YouTube because it's all handled for you but, from a passive income standpoint, YouTube places ads before, potentially after, or in between your videos, they could do banner ads on your videos, there could be pre-roll and post-roll ads, if you do a very long piece of content there could be mid-roll ads that are just like the ads in between television shows,

So you could do that and it can be lucrative, there are some creators who don't make a lot of money per view with it, and there are others that make an extraordinary amount of money per thousand views with.

But the thing that I want to caution you on is if you want to go there and you want to make money, you have to consider whether the genre and niche that you're playing in is one that has money to back it in the form of the advertisers,

So you'll want to do some research there.

But it is a valid way to make passive income and you could make a couple thousand dollars a month directly off the advertisers.

That's not counting active income in terms of sponsorships, live donations via chats that happen through what YouTube calls Super Chat...etc.

There are so many ways to make money on YouTube, and the other great thing about YouTube is that YouTube could be a distribution and marketing funnel for you to sell your other digital products,

whether that's your print on demand products,

whether it's your online courses,

whether it's the digital products,

whether it's the affiliate marketing,

the referral sales,

you can sell all of that,

there's so many ways to leverage that through YouTube and through podcasting, blogging, or Instagram that is ridiculous.

This actually brings us to :

Number VI

# Merchandise

# Merchandise

By selling your own merchandise, your own t-shirts, or hats or whatever, you can actually make substantial revenue from your existing audience and the thing is, I like Instagram for this almost as much if not more than YouTube and yes, I'm aware to make real money with this, you will have to build an audience once again.

I think you should be doing that anyway, I don't think that should be a barrier for you.

The great thing is with merchandise, though, is people don't even have to be so insanely enamored to the content if the shirts are cool enough.

So, just make a dope t-shirt and you're good to go and, like I said, you can put marketing behind this.

I think Instagram is undervalued not only as a content marketing platform that can result in real sales but also people refuse to do even a modest advertising spend in order to put money in and make more money on the backend.

So, I really think that that's something you should look into.

So far we've covered making your own digital products, we've talked about making print on demand products, we've talked about merchandise, we've talked about YouTube, we've talked about affiliate sales, and we've talked about referral sales.

Let's talk about royalties.

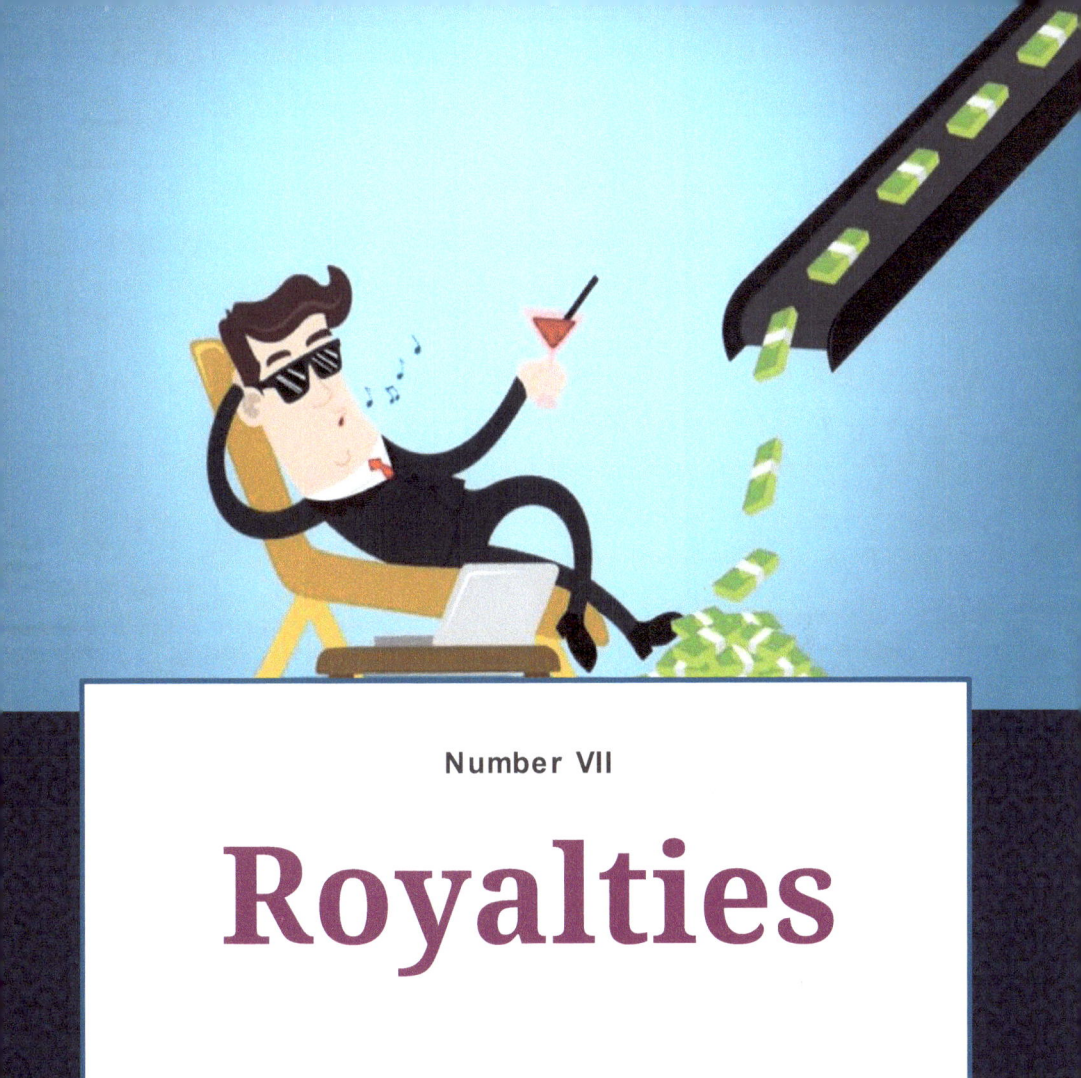

Number VII

# Royalties

# Royalties

There are a lot of ways you could make royalties and that's something you should think about.

Royalties are earnings you get when you license content and the thing is, it doesn't have to be a course.

You could do this with music, videos...etc.

There are so many ways to do licensed content.

And here's another thing that can tie into royalties,

let's talk about stock media,

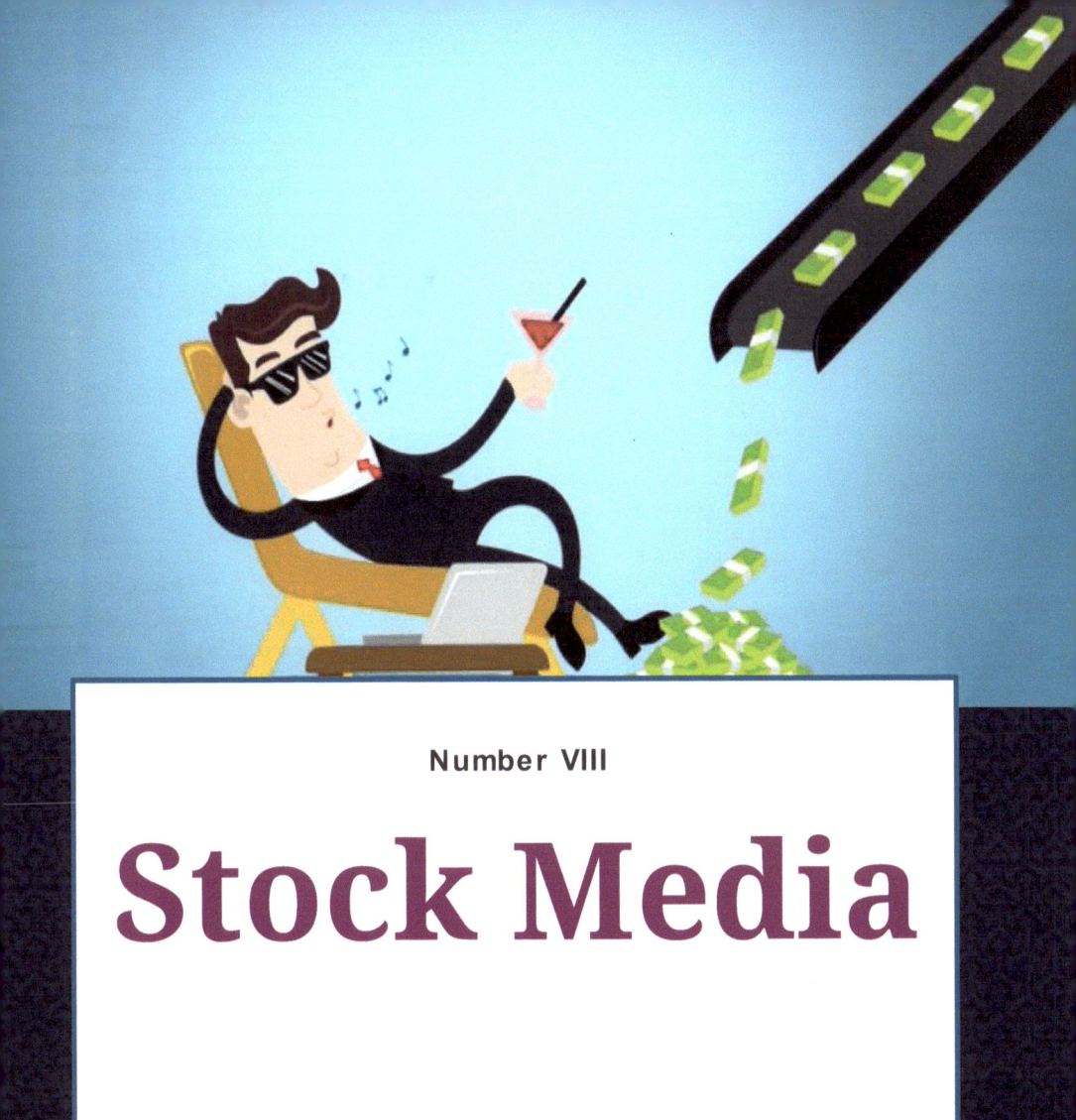

Number VIII

# Stock Media

# Stock Media

By doing stock media licenses : images, video, and audio. You have the ability to go to all of these different platforms that those things are distributed on and marketers and advertisers and creators could buy those things and you will get a commission, you will get a cut of that.

So, you know, you're paying for the distribution on the backend of, you know, them taking some of the money up front but you're making sales you'd never make on your own because, as we pointed out, building an audience is hard, getting traffic is hard.

I'm gonna recommend Black Box because with Black Box, it automatically distributes you to multiple stock websites so you don't have to re-upload the same assets over and over again, so this is a very good way for you guys to make passive income off of things you might already have sitting on your hard drive, you might already have images, graphics, photos, video that are going to waste that somebody could take advantage of and you could make money off of.

And now let's talk about something else.

Let's talk about E-books

Number IX

# E-books / Audiobooks

# E-books / Audiobooks

Right this moment but a lot of people have benefited from this and they've inspired me to tackle this one and that is going to be E-books and Audiobooks.

With E-books and Audiobooks, the thing that intrigues me is that with an ebook, there's the opportunity to link out to resources and to tie it to the last way of making passive income which is email marketing which I'm gonna go deeper into, but with your ebook, you can link out to the opportunity for email marketing by offering free downloads in the E-book or the Audiobook and resources that go to that and in exchange someone has to give you their email address.

Now that you've captured that email address, you can give them the free things that they signed up for but you can also put them into an automated email sequence that could market to them in other ways and through this email marketing, you have the ability to passively, through a system, to potentially sell them your existing digital download products, your print on demand products, your merchandise, your online course, affiliate links to things that fit the thing that they asked for in terms of the value proposition, so every other form of passive income for the most part that we discussed is now accessible through the distribution of email marketing because we're talking about building a system here.

So, by building this system, by building this ecosystem of having all of these diverse revenue streams or a few of them or the ones that fit you and then being able to tie that to content marketing, email marketing, or even online advertising, you have the ability to grow this even bigger and so that's how people really make a living off of passive income.

It's not something they do overnight,

It's not something they do in 30 days,

It's not something they do in 60 days.

This is a long haul incremental process and I wanted to walk you through that and I wanted to give you a little bit more insight and depth into how it actually works.

Number X

# Stocks

# Stocks

Stocks are one of the best ways to earn passive income online but they do require a hefty initial investment,

But, if you have the funds then you should not overlook this opportunity as it would help you earn real passive income for years to come,

I think we actually covered quite a few legitimate ways to make passive income online.

This is something that I feel is accessible to more of you than you might be thinking.

There are a lot of you who already have a skill, there are a lot of you who already have knowledge and the thing is, building an audience is something that you can do.

It's not something that isn't on the table.

You might be the person who learns and benefits from this, and there are people who are gonna learn and benefit from your online course.

I want you to stop thinking and I want people to stop having this conversation that passive income is somehow a scam or it's scummy or it's a daydream or it's for the people who are lazy.

It's for people who are smart and, for people who respect and value their time, It's for people who want to start a family.
It's for people who want to spend more time for their family.
Or, it's for people who don't feel they've been respected and earned what their knowledge is worth in traditional and conventional means and jobs.

So, if that's someone like you, then I hope that this book was helpful and I hope it helps you take your first steps toward either some extra money on the side or real financial freedom.

If You Liked This Book Then Make Sure To Check My Other Books